A DAY THAT CHANGED AMERICA

D-DAY

JUNE 6, 1944

This Scholastic edition is only available for distribution through the school market.

1 3 5 7 9 10 8 6 4 2

ISBN 1-895892-41-4

Printed in Singapore

A DAY THAT CHANGED AMERICA

D-DAY

They Fought to Free Europe from Hitler's Tyranny

TEXT BY SHELLEY TANAKA ❧ PAINTINGS BY DAVID CRAIG

Historical consultation by Joseph Balkoski

A SCHOLASTIC / MADISON PRESS BOOK

SIXTY YEARS LATER, THEY ALL REMEMBER THE NOISE. THE SCREAM OF THE shells whizzing overhead. The drone of the planes heading for the battlefront. The unmistakable fast stutter of an enemy machine gun. The skull-rattling thunder of the big battleship guns.

But even beneath the clamor they could still hear the smaller human sounds. The shouts of a commanding officer. The surprised cry of a struck comrade. The moans of wounded men.

It was the noise of war.

The sounds of D-Day — the greatest invasion in the history of warfare.

CHAPTER ONE

NORMANDY, FRANCE JUNE 6, 1944

It was a bold plan. American, British, and Canadian troops would invade France in a surprise attack. In a single day the Allies would take out the German defenses overlooking the Normandy beaches and secure a base on the continent. From there they would push Hitler out of France, take back Europe, and win the war.

It began just after midnight on June 6, 1944, when 17,000 Allied paratroopers were dropped behind enemy lines to seal off both ends of the beaches. Within a short time, British and Canadian paratroopers took control of bridges and destroyed a powerful German gun battery on the east end of the beachhead.

On the western flank, however, the American paratroopers faced major difficulties.

THE THROBBING ENGINE OF THE PLANE BEAT like a drumroll inside Don Jakeway's head. It drowned out all other sounds. Most of all, it drowned out the roar of the other planes — eight hundred C-47s in all — carrying thousands of American paratroopers to Normandy.

Don looked around at the seventeen other men sitting on benches along both sides of the plane — all members of the 508th Parachute Infantry Regiment of the 82nd Airborne Division. White, ghostly eyes stared out from faces blackened with soot or shoe polish to make them less visible in the dark.

It was just after midnight. Some guys were pretending to sleep. That was a joke. In a few minutes they would be jumping out of the plane, straight down into enemy territory.

Don was twenty years old. Two years ago he was just graduating from Monroe High in Johnstown, Ohio. Life had been school, football, and chores on the family farm. Until one day that summer, outside the local ice cream parlor, when a kid from a rival school pulled out two applications for the airborne forces of the U.S. Army.

(Above) An airplane carrying U.S. paratroopers heads for Normandy. (Inset) The shoulder patches of the two American airborne divisions. (Opposite) Don Jakeway trained for months before parachuting into France early on D-Day.

D-Day and World War II

The long road to D-Day began eleven years earlier when Adolf Hitler (above, inset) and his Nazi party gained power in Germany. Many Germans had felt humiliated by their country's defeat in 1918 at the end of World War I. In fiery speeches at mass rallies Hitler convinced them that the German nation could be great again. After he became chancellor in 1933, Hitler's Nazis began to arrest or eliminate anyone they believed stood in their way, especially Jews, for whom Hitler had a particular hatred.

Hitler also began building up the German armed forces, and threatening neighboring countries. Many people in Great Britain and the United States were alarmed by Hitler's aggression. But no one wanted war. Then on September 1, 1939, Hitler invaded Poland, a country Britain and France had pledged to defend, and so World War II began.

With Italy and Japan, Germany had formed a military alliance known as the Axis. By June of 1940, France had been defeated, and Great Britain seemed on the brink of German invasion. In the months that followed, Britain survived, but Hitler's troops spread over Western Europe and the U.S.S.R. (Russia).

Many Americans thought the United States should stay out of the war in Europe. But on December 7, 1941, when Japan launched a surprise attack on the American navy base at Pearl Harbor, Hawaii, the United States joined Britain and its allies in the battle against the Axis powers.

By June of 1944, the Nazis still controlled much of Europe (above) even though the Russians were advancing westward and the Allies were moving up the boot of Italy. To prevent an attack on the mainland, Hitler had built an "Atlantic Wall" — fortifications that ran from Norway down along the coast of France. He knew D-Day was coming. But he didn't know exactly where — or when.

"Hey, tough guy," the kid had said. "Want to be a paratrooper?"

"Sure," Don had replied. He hadn't even known what a paratrooper was.

He found out soon enough. Paratroopers were the guys who threw themselves out of airplanes with 150 pounds of gear on their backs. They had to be young, single, strong, and brave. They were the first men to go behind enemy lines. From the moment they left the plane, they were on their own. They had to think fast, stay calm, and react quickly to any emergency. A chute that failed to open. Being shot at by enemy fire. Landing in deep water, in a weed-infested swamp, in a tree.

Training to be a paratrooper was the hardest thing Don had ever done. He had learned how to crawl under machine-gun fire and around exploding charges, how to sprint through the woods and shoot at pop-up targets. He had bulked his 138-pound body up to 180 pounds and worked out until he could do twenty-five deep knee bends with a grown man slung over his shoulder.

These snapshots show paratroopers during their practice jumps in England in the spring of 1944.

And he had learned how to jump. First from towers — 35 feet, 60 feet, and then 250 feet above the ground. And finally from a plane. After five jumps he got his wings. Not many did. For every 2,500 men who signed up for the Airborne, only 120 made it to become paratroopers.

Some of the men said they loved the beauty of the fall, feeling so free and so focused at the same time. Don just liked the relief he felt when his chute actually opened and he

The *D* in D-Day

When most people hear the term *D-Day*, they think of June 6, 1944. *D-Day* was the official word used to identify the day that American, British, and Canadian forces invaded Normandy, France. But D-Day is also the general military term that refers to the day any planned attack will take place. In fact, there have been many other D-Days in history since the term was first used in World War I. The D in D-Day doesn't stand for anything, although many people connect it to the words "decision," "departure," or "disembarkation." Naming an invasion day D-Day enables leaders to make plans without speaking about specific dates. This helps keep the chosen invasion date a secret from the enemy. The days following D-Day are given as D+ the number of days (for example, D+4 means four days after D-Day).

hit the ground. There was nothing beautiful about it. They had been taught to hit and tumble before springing to their feet. He usually landed like a bag of potatoes, and when he dragged himself to his feet, every muscle in his body hurt.

Six months ago they had shipped out, to Northern Ireland and then to Nottingham, England. Don remembered how excited he had been when he first saw Sherwood Forest from the train window. Robin Hood country. Before he joined the military, he had never been more than fifty miles from his hometown.

Now he would be seeing real action for the first time. He was part of the largest airborne invasion in history.

During the next few hours, in the black of night, American airborne divisions would land in a small area at the west end of the Normandy beaches. At the east end, British paratroopers would do the same thing. Once they landed, they were to find the other members of their unit, seize the bridges and road crossings, and stop German reinforcements from coming onto the beaches. Then, at daybreak, thousands of British, Canadian, and American ground troops would invade the beaches from the sea.

It was a risky plan, but they were ready. For the past week they had been fenced inside camps and airfields, studying maps and aerial photos and memorizing Normandy landmarks. Don had checked his chute and equipment over and over again. Helmet, life preserver, gas mask. M-1 rifle and bandoliers of ammo, revolver, hand grenades, and trench knife. Compass, maps, French money. Canteen, first-aid kit, food, cigarettes, extra socks, toilet paper. Half-pound blocks of TNT to blow up a bridge or railroad crossing.

When the invasion was postponed a day because of bad weather, they all thought they were going to go mad with the waiting. They were all wound up. There were fights in the barracks. One soldier threw a live grenade out of a hangar after he pulled out the pin and couldn't get it back in.

Then tonight, just before the paratroopers got on the planes, the Red Cross girls had handed out coffee and doughnuts, and they had all gorged themselves silly, even stuffing doughnuts in their pockets.

That may have been a mistake, Don thought now, as the bouncing of the plane made the coffee and doughnuts slosh around inside him. He was sweating. Their jumpsuits had been sprayed with a special coating as protection against poison gas, and it felt as if he were wearing a plastic raincoat. He struggled to his feet and made his way to the open door.

The night was clear, the moon out. It was magnificent to see the hundreds of planes around him, their wings painted with broad black and white identification stripes. They looked like a flock of exotic steel birds.

Fooling the Enemy

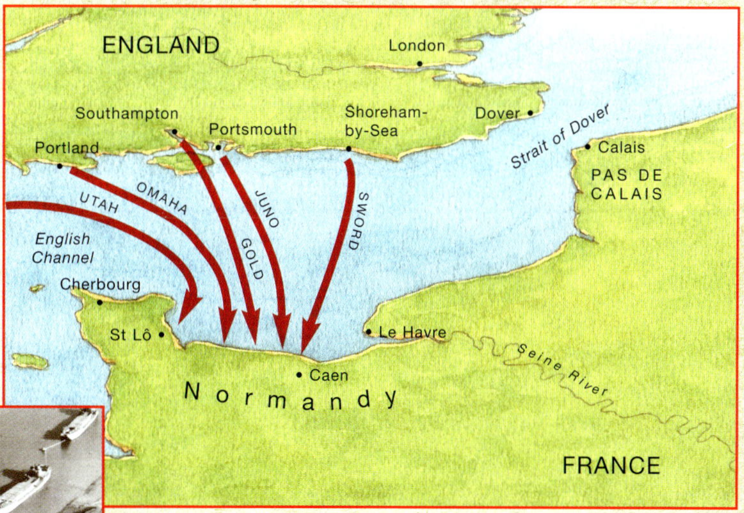

Hitler believed the Allies would invade at the Pas de Calais (right), the English Channel's narrowest point. But the Normandy beaches (code-named Utah, Omaha, Gold, Juno, and Sword) were less well defended, and the possibility of surprise was greater.

To keep the enemy from guessing the actual location and date of the invasion, a massive deception campaign was launched, called Operation Fortitude. The plan included the creation of phantom armies, complete with names and insignias (right), as well as inflatable tanks, jeeps, and ships (above) that could be assembled or dismantled quickly. From the air the dummy equipment looked real, and enemy planes flying overhead were fooled into thinking that troops were massing at locations other than England's south coast.

As they approached the coast, however, thick fog blanketed the plane.

No one could tell that the pilots were widening their formation to avoid colliding with one another. No one could tell that they were veering off course.

As the clouds broke, Don suddenly saw an explosion just ahead. It was his first sight of enemy fire. He returned to his seat and promptly threw up.

That got everyone's attention. His fellow soldiers yelled at him in disgust, and many immediately got sick themselves.

A red light went on beside the door.

"Stand up and hook up!" The command from the jumpmaster drove all other thoughts from his mind as the men hooked up to the static line that would pull open their chutes.

Don was second in line. Outside he could see antiaircraft fire whizzing by, rockets exploding in the air. It looked as though they were flying through the biggest Fourth of July celebration ever.

The green light came on.

"Let's go, men. Good luck," the jumpmaster said, and then they were out the door, one after another, just as they had been trained to do.

Don jumped. At first he just fell like a stone. He remembered everything he had been taught. He fought the urge to reach up and hang on to something before the slack of the chute was taken up. He kept his hands in so they didn't get tangled, and so he could pull his reserve chute if he had to. He kept his head down so the metal buckles didn't hit him in the back of the head when his pack opened.

Don's parachute opened with a painful jolt. It felt as if his shoulders were being ripped off. For forty seconds he floated down. He tried to catch sight of the bundle of supplies and machine guns that had been dropped from the belly of the plane, but he couldn't see it. The sky was alive with fire from German defenders. Directly below him he could see the silvery gleam of open water. Don knew the Germans had flooded the low fields behind Utah Beach to stop the invaders from moving inland. He also knew that if he landed in deep water with his heavy equipment, he would drown. Desperately, he pulled his chute to one side to avoid the floodland.

(Opposite) As the green light flashes, Don Jakeway braces himself before jumping into the night sky over Normandy. Because of heavy enemy gunfire, the planes were flying at almost double their normal speed when the paratroopers exited the aircraft.

He landed in a tree in a churchyard. It was not a good place to be, stuck and in full view of the Germans. He quickly pulled his trench knife out of his boot. It seemed to take hours to cut himself out of his chute. Then he dropped to the ground, fixed his bayonet to his rifle, and made a dash for the nearest hedgerow.

Not far away he could hear the splatter of gunfire. He began to creep along the base of the hedgerow. The tangled ridges of rocks, roots, thorns, and trees were as thick as a fortress wall. The field he was in was empty, but he knew German troops could be waiting just on the other side of the ridge.

Don thought of using his cricket — the small clicker each paratrooper had been given so that they could identify one another in the dark. But he decided it might also reveal his position to the enemy, so he threw it away. Then he set off to find his unit, walking in the direction of the firing.

A replica of a cricket like the one Don Jakeway was issued.

As he passed alongside a stone wall, he suddenly heard footsteps. He clambered over the wall and slid down a slope on the other side, straight into a pile of fresh cow dung. He sat there, barely breathing, as German voices and the tramp of an enemy platoon went by on the other side. He waited for a long time, even after the sounds had passed.

He was still following the wall when he heard a sudden swishing noise. He looked up and ducked as giant wings sailed by only a few feet above his head. It was an American glider. Like a grounded kite, it skidded over the furrows and crashed into a hedgerow on the other side of the field.

Don knew the glider might contain anything from anti-tank guns and radios to jeeps, baby bulldozers, or even fellow soldiers. He sure would have welcomed the sight of an American face.

But when he went over to investigate, he saw that the glider was hopelessly mangled, all the men inside dead.

It was only a matter of time until the Germans came to investigate the crash. So he hurried back to the cover of the hedgerow. Then he took out the trench tool that hung from his belt and dug a narrow slit in the ground.

All U.S. servicemen carried portable supplies of food, such as this can of bread.

He opened one of his cans of K-rations — ham and eggs — and put something in his stomach. He examined his food supply. Two more cans of K-rations, candy bars, biscuits, bouillon cubes, coffee, sugar. He was glad he had traded his cigarettes for extra bouillon and chocolate. It might be a long time before he met up with his fellow troops.

Dawn was breaking. He decided he would hide and get some sleep. Then he would continue to follow orders.

Find his unit. And avoid being killed by the Germans.

A replica paratrooper hangs today from the church spire in Ste-Mère-Eglise. It is a tribute to all the Allied paratroopers and Private John Steele, who was snagged there on June 6, 1944.

DON HAD NO WAY OF KNOWING THAT AT that very moment, thousands of American paratroopers were scattered over the fields and marshes around him. Many were miles from their intended drop zones. Some had left the planes so close to the ground that their parachutes did not have time to open. Many were shot in the air, their chutes bursting into flames as they crashed to the ground. One paratrooper was caught on the steeple of a village church and hung there for hours pretending to be dead to avoid being shot. Some had drowned in the marshes, pulled to the bottom by the weight of their equipment. Others tried to hack their way out of the weeds using their knives.

Many of the radios the commanders needed were lost or damaged in the water. With no means of communicating with one another, the small pockets of paratroopers had no way of knowing where their fellow soldiers were. Worst of all, no one knew whether the beach landing was succeeding, or whether the Allied paratroops were now completely stranded behind enemy lines.

CHAPTER TWO

IN THE AIR

At the same moment that paratroopers were dropping behind enemy lines, Allied fighter and bomber pilots were preparing to take off from air bases in England. Before dawn, thousands of planes would head across the Channel to bomb German troops and defenses. With luck, the weakened German forces would be unable to withstand an attack on the beaches at dawn.

THE ROOM WAS DEADLY QUIET. QUENTIN AANENSON LOOKED AT THE FACES OF THE THIRTY other fighter pilots sitting around him. Only minutes before, the men had been wakened in their barracks and told to report to the briefing room.

They glanced at one another — a sea of pale, serious faces. No one spoke.

The commander walked to the front of the room. He pulled aside a black curtain to reveal a map and pointed to an area called Normandy.

Before the war, Quentin hadn't even known where Normandy was.

"Gentlemen," the commander said. "This is it."

No one had to ask what he was talking about. England had been an armed camp for weeks, filled to bursting with tanks, trucks, artillery, planes, ships, and supplies. Now three million soldiers, sailors, and airmen were waiting to take part in the invasion of France. If the operation was successful, the Allies would retake Europe, and Hitler would be defeated.

Quentin was just twenty-two years old, and although he had trained as a fighter pilot, he had

Fighter pilot Quentin Aanenson, dressed in regulation leather bomber jacket, cap, and goggles.

never flown a combat mission before. Now he was going to be part of the biggest invasion in the history of warfare.

The commander briefed the men on their objectives and targets. They would be leaving within two hours. Quentin wrote down the Start Engine and Takeoff times on the inside of his left wrist. The pilots synchronized their watches. It was just an hour past midnight.

The weather conditions were poor. There was wind and cloud cover over Normandy. The pilots might have to fly low to see their targets, making them easy marks for German antiaircraft gunners.

Out on the runway, the roar was deafening as the crew chief gave the signal to start engines. Dust filled the air.

Quentin followed the other P-47s as they taxied out in takeoff order. The nose of the Thunderbolt was so big that he had to weave his head back and forth to see past it.

This was it. He felt as though everything he had ever done was in preparation for this precise moment. The whole world had been waiting for this day.

He thought of Jackie, his fiancée. Across the ocean in Louisiana she was getting ready for bed at this very moment, probably writing a letter to him, the way she did every day.

Then he shook off all thoughts of home and concentrated on the task at hand. He was a combat fighter pilot, and this was his first mission. He just prayed that he would not mess up.

He revved his motor and checked his controls. He locked the tail wheel into position and waved to his wingman. Then he pushed the throttle forward.

Quentin had wanted to be a fighter pilot ever since the war started. As a high school senior he had watched newsreels of the mighty German tanks advancing through Europe. He saw handsome young RAF pilots flying their Spitfires and Hurricanes with skill and courage. When the opportunity came to join up and go to flight school, Quentin had leaped at the chance. He thought it would be a thrilling way to fight the war.

And it was true that there was nothing like it. Flying the world's biggest and fastest fighter plane to the edge of its limits — dive-bombing, looping, and climbing, all alone in the cockpit. It made his heart race. He felt like the king of the skies.

But you were on your own if things went wrong, too, and there were many ways a fighter pilot could die. Bad weather, carelessness, or simple bad luck. Being caught in the explosion of your own bombs and burning to death in the cockpit. Blacking out after a steep dive. If you were hit by enemy fire, there was no copilot to help you get back to base. If your wounds were too serious for you to be able to fly or bail out, you simply crashed and died. Some pilots had nervous breakdowns from the enormous pressure of the job. Going flak happy, they called it.

The coast of England faded behind him, and Quentin joined his squadron in formation. As they headed over the English Channel, the broad white stripes on their wings gleamed in the moonlight. Then the cloud cover broke, and for a few seconds Quentin looked down at the sea below.

In every direction, moving soundlessly through the black water, were ships of all shapes and sizes — battleships, cruisers, destroyers, and landing craft. Barrage balloons hovered above the fleet. It was a magnificent sight, like watching a herd of slow-moving beasts swimming through the water.

Then the fog covered the sea again, blanketing the coastline that lay straight to the south and forcing the planes to come in dangerously low, right over the German guns.

Quentin's squadron flew over the Normandy coast almost at ground level. The leader spotted their target — German artillery positions and troop concentrations to the left. The lead plane leaned, rolled almost upside down, and zeroed in. Just seconds apart, the other planes in the group followed and attacked.

Quentin pushed the handle to release his bombs, and the plane sprang up with the loss of the weight. He quickly pulled back the throttle and climbed to the left to avoid being caught in his own blast.

Then the fighters swung back in again. This time Quentin blasted away with the eight .50-caliber machine guns mounted on his wings. As the guns kicked back, firing dozens of rounds in seconds, the plane slowed abruptly, and there was a terrible roar on both sides.

Then they pulled up, reassembled in formation, and turned to make the trip back to England.

It was all over in minutes — so quickly that Quentin couldn't even tell whether he had hit his target. But his squadron had lost no planes, and only three or four had flak damage.

If the bombers had done their job, the German defenses would be weakened when the invasion came by sea. At dawn, thousands of landing craft would hit the beaches, and a mighty army of troops and tanks would swarm onto enemy soil.

(Opposite) Quentin Aanenson flies his Thunderbolt P-47 over the coast of Normandy in the early hours of D-Day. The rugged, well-armed Thunderbolt was the Air Force's best fighter-bomber.

K8

Outside Jackie Greer's window, the city buses were still grinding down the streets of Baton Rouge, Louisiana. It was almost midnight on June 5, but Jackie wanted to finish her letter to Quentin. Besides, there was a war on, and the days didn't seem long enough to contain all the things there were to do.

All across the country, people were pitching in to help the war effort. Families grew their own vegetables in "victory gardens" so that farmers could concentrate on feeding the troops. Volunteers rolled bandages and collected scrap metal and rubber. Gas was rationed, so people drove less or shared their vehicles. When the army needed more phone lines, people were happy to deliver messages to neighbors. When there were no nylon stockings to be had, women smeared their legs with tan makeup. Some even drew fake seams down the backs of their legs with an eyebrow pencil. Jackie's mother spent her ration coupons carefully, and her recipe book was filled with cheerful notes about how to manage with less sugar or butter.

Throughout the war, many American women worked in factories that manufactured firearms, machinery, and vehicles needed by troops overseas. (Left) A woman inspects rifle and machine-gun bullets. Beside her is a photograph of her husband, a soldier in the U.S. Army. (Right) Banners honoring America's fighting men were hung in many homes throughout the country.

When the war broke out, Jackie was at college studying home economics. But with the men off fighting there were plenty of jobs available for women in offices and on military bases. One day her father brought home an old typewriter and plunked it on the dining-room table. Jackie and her sister took turns practicing their typing during every spare moment, and when they were fast enough they got jobs working in the offices at Harding Field, where the fighter pilots trained.

That's where she had met Quentin, and now her life revolved around the air base. She knit sweaters for the airmen. She helped organize dances for the officers and enlisted men. And every Sunday the airmen swarmed into town to go to church because they knew that some family would invite them home for Sunday dinner. Mrs. Greer's fried chicken was famous, and the Greers were always happy to open their home to soldiers.

Jackie loved working at Harding. Her office was right in the hangar, and she could look out huge picture windows and watch the P-47s taxi by. She would imagine that Quentin was in one of them. Sometimes she wished she could dig a little hole behind his seat and fly with him on his missions.

They all knew the Allies were preparing for an invasion. When something big happened, Quentin would be part of it.

In the meantime, life was busy and intense. Every morning Jackie grabbed the paper and read the news first instead of the funnies. After work she would rush to the mailbox to see whether there was a letter from Quentin. Sundays were bad. There was no mail delivery on Sundays. But then she could hope for two letters on Monday to make up for it. When she wasn't working or volunteering, there were basketball games and midnight movies and horseback riding and dances and weddings.

And in every spare moment she wrote it all down for Quentin, so he would know there was a world waiting for him after the terrible business of war was over.

Commanding the Invasion

General Dwight D. Eisenhower (below) was the supreme commander of the Normandy invasion. Although he was advised and supported by British, American, and Canadian generals, it was up to him to make the final decisions.

One of the most critical decisions was the timing of the invasion. Since an early June date was necessary to take advantage of favorable tides and a full moon, the invasion was originally set for June 5. But that day the Channel seas were extremely choppy, and the skies too windy, so the invasion was postponed. Early on the morning of June 5, Eisenhower decided that even though the seas would still be rough, the Allies would invade at dawn on June 6. Any further delay would jeopardize the secrecy of the mission.

Eisenhower knew the invasion could go either way. On D-Day, he carried in his pocket a speech that he would read if the invasion did not succeed. In it, he took full blame for the failed attack.

The success of D-Day made Eisenhower a hero, especially at home, and in 1953 he became the thirty-fourth president of the United States.

CHAPTER THREE

ON THE BEACHES

Throughout the night, the mighty armada plowed through the black waters of the English Channel. Near dawn, as 125,000 troops prepared to storm the Normandy coast, the Allied battleships opened fire on the German defenses on shore. Shortly after daybreak, the first waves of troops began landing on the beaches — the British at Sword and Gold, the Canadians at Juno, and the Americans at Omaha and Utah.

Nothing in all his training had prepared seventeen-year-old Bob Giguere for the deafening boom of the big battleship guns. He had never heard or felt anything like it. The roar made the air vibrate. It sent his skull banging against the inside of his helmet.

In the black of night, Bob's ship had crossed the Channel. All around him, vessels of every shape and size stretched as far as the eye could see. The seas were rough, and he was already weak with seasickness as the fleet waited to attack the Normandy beaches.

He found it hard to believe that he'd wanted to join up so badly. His mother had had to sign a special permission form because he wasn't even eighteen. But she let him go. Even though he was the oldest of ten children. Even when his father died shortly after Bob started boot camp. She didn't want her eldest son having to become the man of the house.

But the family was very close, and his brothers and sisters wrote to him all the time. The little ones would send their drawings and scrawls. They drew pictures of ships and explosions because he was a seaman, a demolition expert. They thought he was off on a great adventure.

Some adventure. As the landing craft drew closer to shore, the waters became a heaving stew of noise and confusion. The warships were behind them now, firing over their heads at the German gun emplacements overlooking the beach. From the bluffs, Germans were firing at the waves of troops struggling to make it ashore at Omaha Beach.

It was like running a deadly obstacle course. Just below the water lay giant crisscrossed steel rails waiting to rip open the hulls of the Allied boats. There were stakes topped with mines sticking out of the sand. Farther up the beach were thick barriers of barbed wire and more mines.

Behind that were the German gun emplacements embedded in the bluffs and cliffs above the beach. Omaha Beach was one of the most heavily defended sections on the entire French coast. Along a four-mile stretch, eight hundred German soldiers manned four big guns, thirty-five rocket launchers, thirty-five concrete bunkers, and eighty-five machine-gun nests. And they were all pouring their fire at the American invaders.

(Above and right) American troops in landing crafts head toward Omaha Beach. (Below) Smoke pours from an incoming landing craft moments after it was hit by German machine-gun fire. (Opposite) Seaman 1st Class Bob Giguere of the 6th Naval Beach Battalion.

Bob was standing on the deck of his landing craft when he suddenly heard a loud explosion in the forward compartment. Smoke and badly wounded men came pouring out, and the craft stalled in the water.

They had hit a mine. As German machine-gun fire splattered the side of the vessel like hail on a tin roof, they began to sink.

The ramps on either side of the landing craft were lowered, and a Coast Guardsman wearing bathing trunks and a helmet jumped into the water to string a rope to the beach for the men to hang on to as they waded in. The starboard ramp had been hit and would not drop all the way. Dead and wounded men clogged the port ramp as the boat hit bottom and began to flood.

Bob knew he had to get off. He quickly shrugged off his heavy pack and inflated his life preserver. Then he ran down the half-open starboard ramp and jumped into freezing water up to his armpits.

He was struggling to wade through the rough surf when he suddenly felt something in his left shoulder, like a giant bee sting. He put his hand to it and felt blood, but he kept going until he stumbled out of the water. Desperately, he looked around for cover. Amphibious tanks were supposed to be there to lead the first waves of troops out of the water, shielding the men from German fire.

(Opposite and left) Amid the roar of artillery explosions and enemy fire, the first waves of American troops struggle to get ashore at Omaha Beach. (Below) This inflatable life belt was washed ashore on the beach decades after D-Day.

But few of the big tanks had made it to the beach. Finally he took shelter behind a steel rail that had been exposed by the low tide. He dressed his wound quickly as enemy bullets kicked up sand all around him. When the crackle of fire had passed by, he ran as fast as he could across the beach, looking for a familiar face from his platoon.

He couldn't find one. He wasn't even sure which section of the beach he was on. His rifle was jammed with wet sand.

Behind him men were struggling in the water. Some were swept off their feet by the heavy waves. Some had their life belts fastened around their waists instead of under their armpits, and the weight of their gear turned them upside down in the water. Many drowned. Others cut their way out of their belts and kicked their way to shore, clinging to floating boxes of supplies and equipment.

(Right) A soldier struggles in the deep water near massive obstacles on the shoreline. After the American troops made it to shore (below), they took cover (opposite) as German artillery pounded the beach.

Tanks, men, supplies, bulldozers, and jeeps began to pour onto the beach. But the German gunfire was pinning them down. They could scarcely move to the right or the left, and they certainly couldn't move forward. Bodies began to pile up right in the path of the off-loading troops and tanks. The beachmaster shouted orders through a megaphone. Officers called to their troops to move forward as they led them over the mine-littered flats at the bottom of the bluff. Everything was blanketed in a choking haze of smoke.

Bob made it to the shelter of the seawall and lay there for a while, trying to get his bearings. Nearby, a man was hit as he struggled out of the water, and Bob ran out to help pull him to shore.

He could see that the tide was rising quickly and the beach was becoming narrower, clogged with soldiers trapped between the rising water and German fire. He could see men lying shoulder to shoulder on the beach while more and more waves of troops came up from behind.

And for the first time, he understood that he might not come out of this day alive.

On Utah Beach, Jack Fox heard the shouts of the captain rising above the wind and the waves as hundreds of landing craft tried to edge in closer to shore. He was part of the 1st Battalion, 8th Infantry Regiment, 4th US Infantry Division. In the overcast dawn, everything looked murky and gray — the sea, the beach, the boats, the faces of the men. Four-foot waves swamped the open landing craft bobbing and rolling in the heavy seas. Jack was drenched, and he hadn't even hit the water yet.

His craft bumped against a sandbar about twenty yards out. The coxswain thought they had reached the beach, so he let down the ramp.

Jack scrambled off and suddenly found himself in water up to his neck. He struggled to shore, his heavy pack weighing him down, his feet like lead on the soft sand. He knew he had to hold on to his medical equipment at all costs. The seventy-pound canvas bag contained the things he needed to do his job — sutures, scissors, antiseptic, sulfa, water-purifying tablets, splints, bandages, plasma, and the precious metal box of morphine.

He had never planned to become a combat medic. It had all been a matter of chance. Like millions of other young Americans, he had been drafted right after high school. At training camp, the new recruits were counted off in groups of twenty and pointed to big tables lined up in a field. Jack had landed at the medic table.

There were all kinds of medics in the army, but combat medics had the most dangerous job. They were given no rifles, so they couldn't defend themselves. Yet medics went into battle with the men on the front lines, the first to walk into enemy fire. And their first duty was to the wounded. They might have to stay behind with an injured soldier while the others retreated or sought cover from the enemy, even though that meant certain capture.

Jack wondered whether he was up to the task. Would he be brave under fire? Could he do his job while the enemy was trying to kill him? They were sure trying to kill him now. All around him the sea was spurting up in little spouts as shells peppered the water. In the smoke and fire of battle no one knew, or cared, that he was a medic. They were simply firing at anything that moved. Still, it felt personal.

Jack finally cleared the water and stumbled onto the beach, weak with the wet and cold and weighed down by his waterlogged clothing and his heavy pack. He knew that if he could make it across the 600-foot stretch to the shelter of the seawall, he could rest, get

Combat medic Jack Fox (opposite) treated dozens of wounded men, like the ones shown at right, during the course of D-Day. (Below) A medic's portable surgical kit included a scalpel, scissors, and a needle and sutures for stitching wounds.

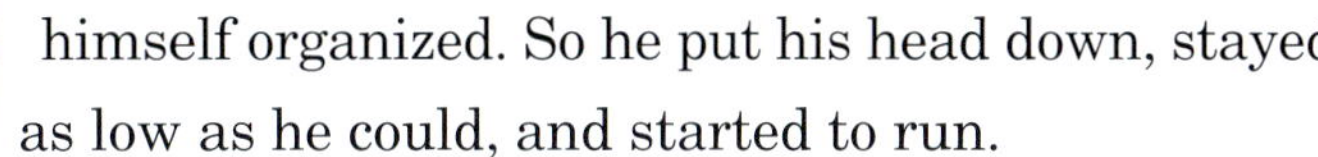

himself organized. So he put his head down, stayed as low as he could, and started to run.

That's when he saw his first casualty. It was a wounded soldier lying on the beach. Jack crouched down and ran over to him, his mind already going through the checklist he had learned in training. *Stop the bleeding. Prevent shock. Tag the soldier. Call the litter men.*

He reached the man and turned him over. He was a friend, and he was dead.

That's when it hit home — the shock, fear, and anger. But there was nothing he could do.

So he picked up his gear and ran to catch up with a general who was gathering the unit together at the seawall.

Brigadier General Theodore Roosevelt, Jr., son of the former president of the United States, informed his men that they had landed in the wrong place. They were a mile south of where they were supposed to be.

"We can't go back and start over," he said. "So we're going to start the war from here." They would forget about trying to move up the beach to their original landing site. They would not wait for new orders. Instead, they would take out the German strongpoints right here. Then, somehow, they would find a path off the beach so they could move inland.

CHAPTER FOUR

MOVING INLAND

As the day wore on, the Allies fought their way off the beaches. Bit by bit, small groups of American troops managed to climb the cliffs and bluffs. By the end of the day they had secured the beaches and pushed a short way inland.

Meanwhile, news of the invasion spread around the world. By midnight, all five beaches were in Allied hands.

EVEN THROUGH THE HAMMERING OF GUNFIRE, BOB GIGUERE COULD HEAR SOMEONE hollering for a demolition man.

Ducking enemy fire mere inches above his head, Bob edged sideways in the direction of the calls. Just beyond the seawall lay a dense barrier of barbed wire that was preventing the American tanks and troops from getting off Omaha Beach.

He went to see what he could do. Two infantrymen had already shoved explosive tubes under the barbed wire and blown a path through the barrier.

Suddenly, an army officer turned to Bob, handed him two egg-shaped grenades and told him to crawl through the opening. After that he was to somehow make his way across a mine-littered antitank ditch. Then he was to throw his grenades and take out an enemy gun emplacement.

Bob wasn't sure why he had been chosen. This wasn't even his unit!

He got down on his hands and knees and crawled on his belly through the gap in the wire. It was at least a hundred yards to the base of the concrete bunker shielding the German guns. But there was a lot of smoke, and it would provide cover if he stayed low.

He scuttled as quickly as he could across the open ground. The last hundred feet felt like a mile. When he got close, he pulled the pins on his grenades and lobbed them into the opening of the gun emplacement.

After that it was like a strange passing game. Bob crouched down below the bunker

(Opposite) At the base of the German bunker, Bob Giguere gets ready to throw his first hand grenade.

while a soldier on the other side of the antitank ditch lobbed a grenade over to him. Then Bob would pull the pin and toss it into the nest. He lost count of the number of grenades, but after at least a half dozen, he was told he had better get out of there in a hurry. The destroyers sitting four miles offshore were scheduled to start shelling at any moment.

He scurried backward at the exact moment that the destroyer's 5-inch guns began firing over his head.

"What's your name, soldier?" the officer said. When Bob asked why he wanted to know, he was told he had just earned himself a medal.

But making it onto the Normandy beaches was just the beginning for the British, American, and Canadian troops. German reinforcements were already heading to the coast to beat back the attackers. If the invasion was going to stick, the Allies had to move inland and stop them.

So Bob followed about fifteen others through a narrow gap across the dunes and up the hill. They moved in single file, carefully stepping in each other's footsteps, because they knew this stretch of beach was full of mines. When they passed the German pillbox for the last time, they tossed in a few more grenades, just for good measure.

An elite unit known as the Rangers accomplished one of the most dangerous assignments on D-Day. They destroyed a German gun battery three miles west of Omaha Beach, set high on a hundred-foot cliff called Pointe du Hoc (left). (Opposite) Advancing American soldiers run for cover behind the hedgerows that lined the sides of the country roads.

The roads and fields behind the beach seemed eerily deserted, the houses and barns quiet. Some buildings were on fire. Shutters were closed up tight, and there was no way of knowing whether a German sniper was waiting behind every door or tree.

They were making their way along a hedgerow lining a cow field when the dreaded words were passed back through the line of soldiers.

"German patrol!"

Bob was handed two grenades. Then they all ran along the hedgerow and silently hid behind a clump of brush and boulders beside the cattle path.

As the German patrol marched past the opening, the Americans heaved their grenades into the next field. The Germans backed up and scattered, and the American riflemen opened fire.

When Bob looked back, he saw two dozen German bodies lying in the field.

About a mile south of the beach, the tiny town of Colleville-sur-Mer was being heavily defended as Bob and his group cautiously advanced. They could see a German gun spotter surveying the village from the tall stone steeple of the church, and they rushed inside to take cover.

Inside the church an American soldier lay dead at the foot of the stairs. A small group of French Resistance fighters were huddled in the corner. But the church was not a safe place to be. Bob could hear the big guns of the battleships and destroyers anchored off the beach. They were aiming their fire at the village just as the first American troops were advancing into town. It was only a matter of time before their sights found the highest rooftop in the village.

As they fled the church, the big guns continued to fire. Within minutes, the stone steeple had been blown away, and the church was rubble.

By late afternoon American jeeps, tanks, and troops were finally beginning to pour inland. But Bob knew he had to find his unit. So, escorting a group of wounded American soldiers, he left Colleville-sur-Mer and made his way down the road back to Omaha Beach.

It was a horrific scene. Below the cliffs, gorse bushes were on fire. The beach was littered with burning jeeps, stranded bulldozers, rifles, crates, life preservers, and corpses. Soldiers picked their way around torn-up bodies floating in the surf. The beach foam was pink in places. Graves Registration men were moving the dead to the side of the beach. When there was no more room, they began to stack the corpses like wood.

Bob stumbled down the beach, trying to find his outfit through the smoke and dust. Everything was gray and yellow, and the air stank of gunpowder.

Suddenly he heard an explosion, very near. For a split second he wondered whether it was from mortar or artillery. Then he lost consciousness and crumpled to the ground.

"MEDIC! OVER HERE!"

All day long the desperate cry rang like a bell in Jack Fox's ears, as the medical teams followed the fighting men inland.

Jack had seen dozens of training films, done hundreds of practice exercises, even participated in a mock invasion in England. But nothing had really prepared him for the terrible wounds of actual combat. Arms and legs blown off, bellies ripped open, faces shot away, shrapnel embedded in necks and arms.

His job was to keep the wounded soldiers alive long enough to be dragged off the field

(Opposite) Jack Fox, right, and fellow medics administer plasma to a badly wounded man to help replenish his blood. Medics treated the wounded as quickly as possible and carried them off the beach on stretchers to get them out of the line of fire.

and transported to a collecting station to receive medical treatment. If a medic could stop the bleeding and prevent a soldier from going into shock, the man had a good chance of recovery.

Again and again Jack cut away bloody clothing and then stopped the bleeding any way he could. He pressed down on spurting arteries, bandaged gaping wounds, tied tourniquets. He sprinkled sulfa powder to help prevent infection, and tied splints onto broken legs and arms so men could be moved. If a soldier needed plasma and Jack couldn't find a vein in the arm, he tried to find one in the ankle. He went through a lot of morphine. Then he pinned the empty morphine tube to the man's jacket or simply wrote *M* on his forehead, in case another medic accidentally killed the man by giving him an overdose. Finally, he wrote a brief description of the man's condition on the emergency medic tag, tied the tag to the soldier with string and left him for the litter bearers. There were supposed to be red tags for the most urgent cases, but they were all urgent.

Many of the men were parched with thirst from blood loss and begged for water. Sometimes the water came from the canteen of a dead comrade lying nearby. Men shivered from shock, but there weren't enough blankets. Sometimes all Jack could do was offer a few words of comfort and light a last cigarette for a dying man. Sometimes there was nothing to do but call the Graves Registration team to deal with the dead.

By the end of the day, there was a chain of wounded flowing from the front lines. Medics, litter bearers, and jeeps swarmed the area like worker ants. They went from one group of wounded to another, carrying them back to clearing stations on the beach. Some men were too badly injured to be moved far, and had to be operated on in makeshift hospitals set up in orchards and farmhouses. Others were evacuated to hospital ships that floated three miles offshore, where surgeons cut and stitched as the ships lurched on the rough seas.

The day continued in a blur as Jack followed his unit inland. He lost track of how many men he had treated. He did not know what time it was, where he was, or even which direction the firing was coming from.

When they finally stopped for the night, they were only about a mile from Utah Beach. They were all too exhausted to move off the road, make camp, eat together. As the darkness deepened, Jack simply dropped into a roadside ditch, shrugged off his pack, and curled into a ball.

The night air was very cold. It suddenly seemed very quiet.

It's going to be a long war, he thought to himself. Then he closed his eyes and let sleep wash over him.

D-Day: The Turning Point in the War

D-Day did not go perfectly for the Allies. But it succeeded, largely because it caught the Germans off guard. Adolf Hitler thought an invasion would take place two hundred miles east at the Pas de Calais, or as far away as Norway.

On June 6, the Germans assumed the weather was too stormy for an Allied attack. And even though German radar detected the Allied armada in the middle of the night, poor communication meant that the Germans were slow to recognize the seriousness of the invasion.

In the week following D-Day, the Germans and Allies both rushed their forces to the battlefront. The Germans lost the race. Their tanks and troops had to move in by roads and rail lines that had already been heavily bombed, while Allied ships continued to pour across the Channel, bringing tanks, troops, and supplies.

EXTRA! GREENSBORO DAILY NEWS EXTRA!

ALLIES LAND IN FRANCE

Heavy Assault Launched On Northwestern Coast

Across the nation, front-page newspaper headlines informed the public of the Normandy invasion.

ACROSS THE ATLANTIC IN BATON ROUGE, LOUISIANA, JACKIE Greer woke up to the sound of the phone ringing. She looked at the clock on her bedside table. It was exactly 5 A.M.

She hurried down the hall. Her father was talking to their neighbor, Mrs. Garon. It was something about the war, the invasion.

She rushed to the living room and turned on the radio.

"…Allied naval forces, supported by strong air forces, began landing Allied armies this morning on the northern coast of France." Then the announcer read a message from General Eisenhower: "The tide has turned. The free men of the world are marching together to victory."

That morning, little work was done in the office at the air base. Everyone stayed glued to the radio. The heaviest fighting, the announcer said, had been on one of the American beaches, but a small group of soldiers had fought their way up the bluffs and secured the beachhead.

At lunch break Jackie went to a special service in the chapel. All across the country, church bells rang as Americans prayed for the Allied forces.

Jackie prayed, too, with relief and hope. The waiting was finally over. The invasion had begun. If it was a success, the war would end, and Quentin would be coming home.

D-Day: The Greatest Invasion

D-Day was a huge effort that succeeded because many nations worked together, sharing their leadership and resources. Although the invasion was led by American, British, and Canadian forces, Allied troops from a number of other countries — including Australia, Belgium, Czechoslovakia, France, Greece, the Netherlands, New Zealand, Norway, and Poland — also played a vital role during D-Day and the Battle of Normandy.

The Allies landed on five beaches along sixty miles of coastline. To the east, British forces faced a mighty counterattack by German panzer tanks. On Juno Beach, Canadian soldiers fought their way inland through heavy fire within half an hour of landing. By the end of the day, British forces on Gold Beach had made their way five miles inland, and the Allies had secured nearly twenty continuous miles of coastline, stretching from Gold to Juno.

1. Sword Beach. One of three beaches assigned to the 2nd British Army on D-Day. Troops landed along its five-mile shoreline at 7:25 A.M.

2. Juno Beach. This was the assault area assigned to the 3rd Canadian Infantry Division of the 2nd British Army. The Canadians were hit with heavy gunfire from German regiments occupying the seafront homes along the beach. Of the 21,000 troops who landed on Juno, there were 1,200 casualties.

3. Gold Beach. One of three beaches assigned to the 2nd

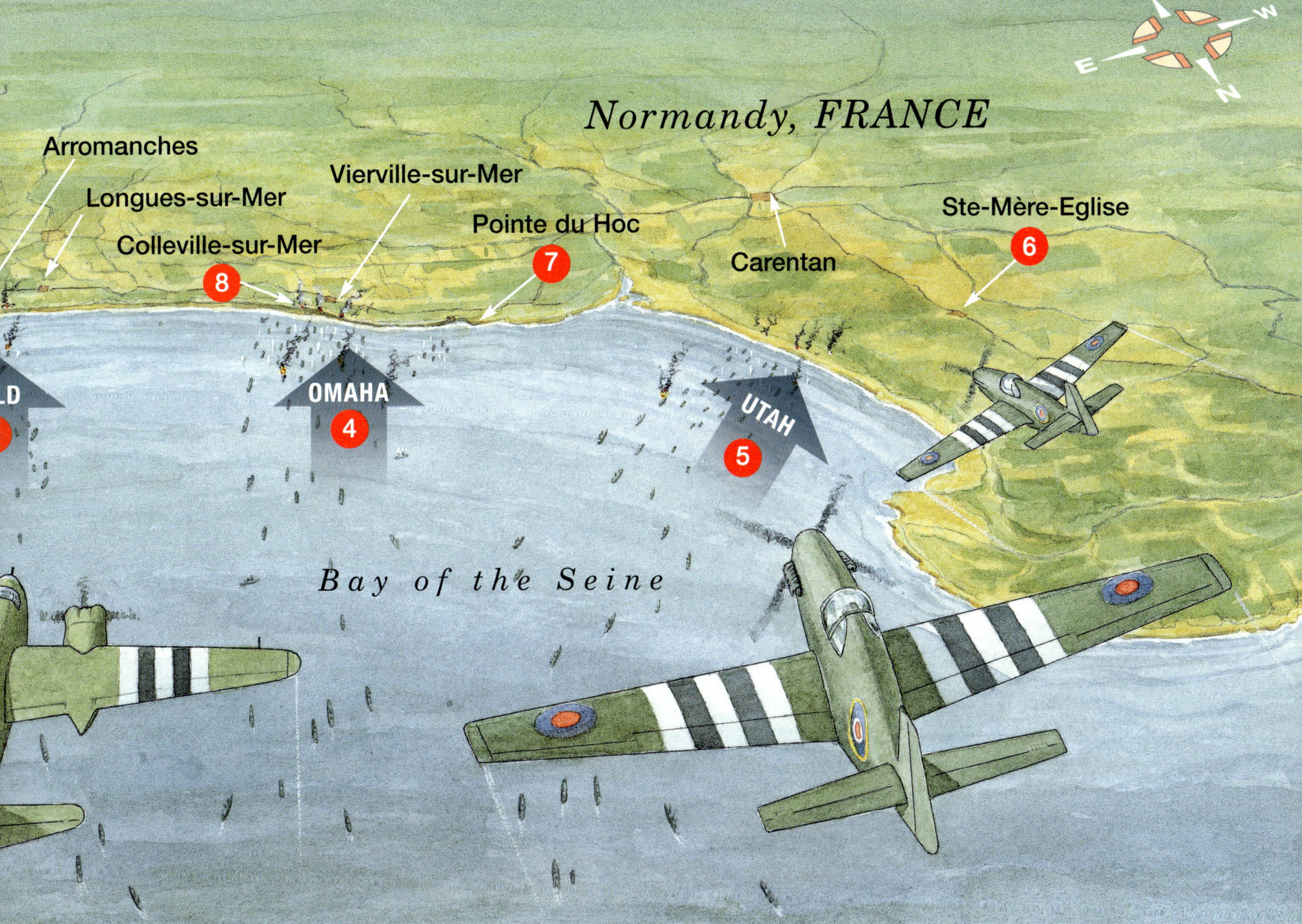

British Army. Despite heavy enemy resistance, the British broke through the coastal defenses and pushed several miles inland by nightfall.

4. Omaha Beach. Nicknamed Bloody Omaha, this four-mile stretch of sand was the largest of the invasion beaches, and it was here that the fiercest fighting of D-Day took place. The waters and beach were heavily mined, and massive Germany artillery was positioned in the 100-foot cliffs overlooking the entire landing area. The American army suffered 4,800 casualties but still managed to land 34,000 troops here by day's end.

5. Utah Beach. Although strong currents, smoke, and underwater mines sent American landing craft about a mile off course, the beach was taken with fewer than 300 casualties.

6. Ste-Mère-Eglise. The American airborne assault concentrated on the area around this town.

7. Pointe du Hoc. A German gun battery was situated a mile or so inland of this 100-foot cliff three miles west of Omaha Beach. The Rangers, an elite unit of the American army, managed to scale the cliff and take out the battery.

8. Colleville-sur-Mer. Bob Giguere took cover in a church in this small French town.

9. Caen. This key city was important to both the Allies and the Germans since all major roads in the area ran through it. The Allies had originally planned to capture Caen by the end of D-Day, but German resistance was too strong. After a month of heavy fighting, the Allies took the city on July 9, 1944. By then, more than eighty percent of Caen had been destroyed.

EPILOGUE

THE GREATEST INVASION

By midnight, the big German guns on the Normandy beaches were silent, and the Allies were safely ashore. There had been more than 10,000 Allied casualties, including close to 8,000 Americans killed, wounded, captured, or missing. Most of those were at what became known as Bloody Omaha, the beach that claimed more lives than any other in the D-Day invasion.

In the days that followed, troops, tanks, and guns continued to cross the Channel. Within a week, the five beaches — Utah and Omaha, plus the three beaches to the east that had been invaded by British and Canadian troops — had been joined up, and the Allies had a firm base on European soil. Although there would be many more months of terrible fighting, the end of the war was in sight. Germany was defeated on May 8, 1945, and World War II finally came to an end when Japan surrendered on August 14 of that same year.

Jack Fox and the other medics and doctors did their jobs well on D-Day. Many wounded men survived, even with horrible injuries. Within a few days, a makeshift airstrip was in place at Omaha Beach, and the lucky ones were being flown back to hospitals in England, where they had access to the latest medical advances.

Since the beginning of the war, scientists had been on a fast track to develop drugs and procedures to repair the terrible damage caused by bullets, shrapnel, and bombs. There were new antibiotics to combat infection, skin transplants to treat serious burns, and advanced plastic surgery techniques.

Jack Fox continued his work as a combat medic after D-Day, moving with the front lines as the invasion forces made their way through France, Belgium, Luxembourg, and Germany. He remained in the army until his retirement as a lieutenant colonel in 1966. He also served as a combat medic in the Korean War.

Four days after D-Day, Bob Giguere woke up in an army hospital in England, his head and body full of shrapnel. It was June 10, 1944 — his eighteenth birthday. After he recovered from his wounds, he continued to serve in the navy, including duty in the jungles of the South Pacific. By the time the war ended, he had been hit once more. Today the shrapnel left in his body still sets off metal detectors in airports when he travels.

Don Jakeway spent four days playing hide-and-seek with the Germans before he finally came across another group of paratroopers, and it was ten days before he rejoined his own outfit. During that time his parents received a telegram from the war department saying their son was missing in action. He continued to fight in Normandy, Holland, Belgium, and Germany, and was wounded twice before he was discharged in 1945.

D-Day was the first of many combat missions for Quentin Aanenson. Ten days after the invasion, he was assigned to the 391st Fighter Squadron of the 9th Air Force. By the time the war ended, he had participated in every major campaign in Western Europe. He had dropped bombs on bridges, railroad trains, and cities, and he had seen many, many people die. He no longer thought being a fighter pilot was thrilling and glamorous. He knew what it was like to fire his machine guns on fleeing German soldiers, circle to count the bodies, and then fly back to the base where he would throw up and then sit alone in his tent reliving the horror of what he had done. He knew how it felt to pack up the lockers of fellow pilots who had died in action.

Like so many American soldiers, sailors, and airmen, Quentin Aanenson returned home from the war a different man. He flinched at loud noises. He couldn't sit still or concentrate long enough to read a few pages of the newspaper. And when gophers dug up the family's fields, he found that he could no longer shoot them. He had seen too much killing.

Quentin and Jackie were married. With her support, the nightmares of the war gradually faded, but they never went away entirely. The memories were burned into his brain, and they left deep scars.

THE MEN WHO SURVIVED D-DAY ARE MOSTLY IN THEIR EIGHTIES NOW. AS EACH DAY PASSES THERE are fewer of them left to tell their stories. Many stay in touch with the men they fought beside. Sharing death is a strong bond.

The war changed Quentin, Don, Bob, and Jack. But it also changed America. Though most countries would spend years rebuilding their cities and their economies, America emerged from the war stronger and richer than ever. The factories and businesses that had been set up to build planes, ships, and guns were now used to produce kitchen appliances, cars, and televisions. People moved around the country, drawn to new jobs and opportunities. The cities and suburbs grew, and wages rose. Women who had taken over for male workers in factories and offices now knew they could do something with their hands besides bake. They discovered what it was like to make money and have jobs outside the home. They also learned what it was like to lose their jobs once the men came home and moved back into the workforce.

Business was booming, and America's years of isolation were over for good. The United States needed to protect its interests — the countries that supplied American industries with natural resources, and the markets that bought American goods. From now on, it would not hesitate to become involved in the affairs of countries around the world whenever American values or interests were threatened.

D-Day was the beginning of the end of World War II. During that war, 13 million Americans served and more than 400,000 Americans were killed. On D-Day the history of the world, and of America, was changed. The war touched every American, and it gave the country a new sense of its place in the world.

(Previous page) A fallen soldier's rifle and helmet mark his temporary grave at Omaha Beach. Today, many nations have war cemeteries honoring the soldiers who were killed in Normandy both on and after D-Day. (Opposite) The American Normandy Cemetery, not far from Omaha Beach, contains 9,386 graves.

GLOSSARY

Allies: the nations, including the United States, Canada, Britain, and the Soviet Union, that fought against the **Axis** powers in World War II.

amphibious: describes an attack involving forces arriving on land from the sea.

artillery: weapons such as large guns and cannons.

Axis: the nations, including Germany, Italy, and Japan, that fought against the **Allies** in World War II.

bandolier: a belt worn over the shoulder and across the chest for carrying ammunition.

bayonet: a sharp steel blade attached to the end of a rifle.

beachhead: a position established by forces after landing on a beach.

bunker: a structure, built of concrete and often dug into the earth, that provides shelter from attacks.

coxswain: a person who steers a boat and is in charge of its crew.

demolition man: an explosives expert.

flak: the bursting **shells** fired from antiaircraft guns.

gun battery/gun emplacement: a defensive position from which weapons are fired.

infantry: soldiers on foot.

litter bearer: one who helps carry wounded soldiers on a stretcher.

mine: a small device hidden in the ground or underwater that is designed to explode when a person or vehicle puts pressure on it.

morphine: a strong pain reliever.

pillbox: a small, low concrete structure from which machine guns are fired.

plasma: the clear-fluid part of blood that helps blood to clot.

RAF: Royal Air Force; Great Britain's air force.

reinforcements: soldiers and supplies sent to strengthen an army.

shells: explosive rounds fired by **artillery**.

shrapnel: metal fragments created by exploding **shells** or grenades.

INDEX

Page numbers in italics refer to illustrations or maps.

PICTURE CREDITS

All paintings are by David Craig unless otherwise indicated. All maps are by Jack McMaster.

C/M — CORBIS/Magmaphoto.com
GCMF — George C. Marshall Foundation, Photos by Joe Swope
NARA — National Archives and Records Administration
NDMF — National D-Day Memorial Foundation

1: GCMF.
6: Courtesy of Donald Jakeway.
7: (Top) Everett Collection/ Magmaphoto.com. (Inset) GCMF.
8: (Inset) Bettmann/C/M.
9: Courtesy of Eric Sykes.
11: (Inset, middle) Imperial War Museum, H42527. (Inset, bottom) U.S. Army Quartermaster Museum, Fort Lee, Va.
14: NDMF.
15: Peter Christopher.
16: Courtesy of Quentin Aanenson.
20: (Left) Bettmann/C/M. (Right) NDMF.
21: NARA.
24: Courtesy of Ken Davey.
25: NARA.
27: (Left) Robert Capa/Magnum Photos. (Inset) April Cheek/ NDMF.
28: (Inset) Robert Capa/Magnum Photos. (Bottom) NARA.
29: Robert J. Rieske/Ohio University.
30: Courtesy of Jack Fox.
31: (Inset) Courtesy of Ken Davey. (Right) NARA.
34: (Left) NARA. (Right) Courtesy of Julie Fulmer.
35: Hulton-Deutsch Collection/C/M.
39: The National D-Day Museum Foundation, Inc.
42–43: NARA.
45: Peter Christopher.

RECOMMENDED READING

For young readers:

D-Day: June 6, 1944 (Days that Shook the World series) by Sean Sheehan (Raintree/Steck Vaughn). Contemporary photographs, maps, and first-person accounts bring this accessible history to life.

The Good Fight: How World War II Was Won by Stephen E. Ambrose (Atheneum). A concise, readable overview of the major events of World War II.

World War II for Kids: A History with 21 Activities by Richard Panchyk (Chicago Review Press). A comprehensive survey of the war, with crafts and activities for readers.

For older readers:

Beyond the Beachhead: The 29th Division in Normandy by Joseph Balkoski (Stackpole Books). A detailed chronicle of life on the front line told with personal accounts.

D-Day, June 6, 1944: The Climactic Battle of World War II by Stephen E. Ambrose (Simon & Schuster). A thorough account and analysis of the Normandy Campaign by the founder of the D-Day Museum in New Orleans and author of *Band of Brothers*.

WEBSITES

The American Experience: D-Day
www.pbs.org/wgbh/amex/dday

Britannica.com, NORMANDY: 1944 search.eb.com/normandy

The National D-Day Museum www.ddaymuseum.org

A Fighter Pilot's Story by Quentin C. Aanenson
pages.prodigy.com/fighterpilot

ACKNOWLEDGMENTS

The author and Madison Press Books would like to thank Quentin Aanenson, Jackie Aanenson, Jack Fox, Robert Giguere, and Donald Jakeway for providing their firsthand accounts of this historic day.

Editorial Director: Hugh M. Brewster
Editorial Assistance: Imoinda Romain
Production Manager: Donna Chong
Associate Editorial Director: Wanda Nowakowska
Graphic Designer: Jennifer Lum
Color Separation: Colour Technologies
Project Editor: Kate Calder
Production Director: Susan Barrable
Printing and Binding: Tien Wah Press

D-DAY was produced by Madison Press Books, which is under the direction of Albert E. Cummings.

Madison Press Books
1000 Yonge Street, Suite 200, Toronto, Ontario, Canada, M4W 2K2